Chocolatey Brown

Stephanie Fleary

ISBN: 0991556305
ISBN 13: **9780991556304**

To all my sun-kissed beauties,
know that you come from
lineage of greatness
and you are a
beautiful
blessing
from
God.

Ms. Honey says I'm a pretty chocolate girl but I'm not quite sure. Does she mean the sweet dark chocolate that Momma buys in the store?

My sister and my cousin don't look quite like I do. They always smile and have lots of fun, doing whatever it is that they do.

6

Ms. Honey says I'm a pretty chocolate girl but some days I'm not quite sure.

Kristopher Jean always laughs at me
and pushes me to the floor.

If only I looked like the girls I see in the fancy magazines, with straight hair like the princesses I see on my TV.

I asked Ms. Honey why she always tells me I'm her pretty chocolate girl. She told me because I'm soft and sweet and the prettiest brown in the world.

My brown is warm and sweet,
like Aunt Mable's chocolate cake.
I guess Ms. Honey has a point
that she is trying to make.

If I believe my chocolate skin is rare
and sweet and good, my chocolate
smell will fill the air just like
Ms. Honey's would.

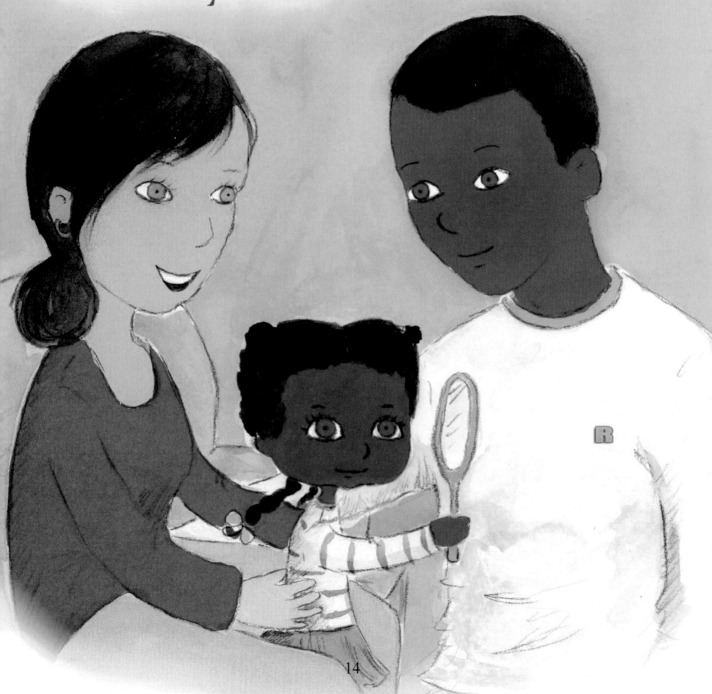

I decided to wake up each day and love my chocolate brown. I smiled much more and laughed for sure never to show a frown.

Kristopher Jean started to play with me and was no longer loud and mean. My sister even read with me and stopped being a mean preteen.

Kaylarose in my gymnastics class asked to play with my hair. She said she wanted braids like mine, having straight hair wasn't fair.

Ms. Honey says I'm her chocolate girl and that's just fine with me.

I'm happy to be who I am,
a pretty sweet chocolatey me.

Words to Know

aura - an energy or invisible quality given off or generated by a person, place or thing

colorism - being treated poorly because of the dark shade of ones skin tone

confident - a feeling or belief that you can do something well or succeed at something

melanin - a dark brown or black substance that is a natural part of people's skin, hair, and eyes

self-esteem - a feeling of having respect for yourself and your abilities

unique - very special

Aunt Mable's Chocolate Cake
Courtesy of Lady Charles Brooklyn, NY

Ingredients

2 cups white sugar

1 3/4 cups all-purpose flour

3/4 cup unsweetened cocoa powder

1 1/2 teaspoons baking powder

1 1/2 teaspoons baking soda

3/4 teaspoon salt

2 eggs

1 cup buttermilk

1/2 cup vegetable oil

2 teaspoons vanilla extract

Instructions

Preheat oven to 350° F. Prepare two 8" or 9"

round pans (or cupcake pans). You can either grease

and flour the pans or use non-stick cooking spray.

In a large mixing bowl, mix together the sugar, flour, cocoa,

baking powder, baking soda and salt.

Make a well in the center of the dry ingredients and add

the eggs, oil, buttermilk and vanilla. Beat for 2 minutes

at medium speed, then stir in the boiling water(or coffee).

Pour into the prepared pans and bake for 30-35 minutes,

or until a toothpick comes out clean.

Allow them to cool for 10 minutes in the pan,

then flip them out on a wire rack and let them completely

cool before frosting.

Chocolatey Brown Pops
Courtesy of Miranda Hayes
Bronx, NY

Ingredients

Chocolate cake (store bought cake mix)	tsp of vanilla
Hershey chocolate instant pudding	water and oil
3 eggs	sprinkles

Instructions

Bake cake in a 9 inch round pan for about 15-20 minutes.
Use a knife to insert into center of the cake and make sure
it comes out clean. Allow cake to cool, crumble cake
into a large bowl and mix with your favorite frosting.
Add enough frosting to get cake to hold together
when rolling. Too much frosting will make cake
too sticky and loose. Best to combine in small amounts.
Roll cake and frosting into equal size balls,
set on wax or parchment paper and allow to chill
in the freezer for about 10-15 minutes.
Melt chocolate disks over double boiler.
Use a toothpick to dip cake balls into chocolate.
After dipping, stick toothpick with cake ball into styrofoam
to dry. Decorate with sprinkles or jimmies while
chocolate is still wet. Carefully remove toothpick from cake ball and enjoy.

"Brown Girl in the Ring"

Popular Caribbean Ring Game
Recorded by Boney M. in 1978

Both young girls and boys hold hands and move around in a circle or ring.

The first player skips around the center. When they sing "show me your motion"

the player does his or her favorite dance, then chooses a friend to join them.

This game is traditionally played in the caribbean and was played

to enhance the children's self esteem.

There's a brown girl in the ring

Tra la la la la

(repeat 2x)

She looks like a sugar in a plum

Plum plum

Show me your motion

Tra la la la la

(repeat 2x)

She looks like a sugar in a plum

Plum plum

Skip across the ocean

Tra la la la la

(repeat 2x)

She looks like a sugar in a plum

Plum plum

Word Search

```
U K P N U E B I E C P T T S L
G Z W W I E Q T F A M M I U N
F J F T L N A J P K E P U B J
B G H I A L A D Q E E F P V U
I V E U O C Q L I F T A V O X
U V R C E O U U E V S E S Q R
E A O V O N Y Q R M E B L E Y
Y H D J X F N B R U F Q X A N
C R L W A I C I Y U L A H Z G
B R O W N D D J O E E U P O K
L R P T G E D V I Z S T W U E
Y F G N T N M S I R O L O C P
C M U V I T U N I Q U E E T W
S Q U A Z Z K J G F R U S D J
R O J P K H V T T A H K T J L
```

AURA   BELIEVE   BROWN

CAKE   CHOCOLATE   COLORISM

CONFIDENT   MELANIN   SELFESTEEM

UNIQUE   25

Help Chocolatey Brown Get to Aunt Mable's Bakery

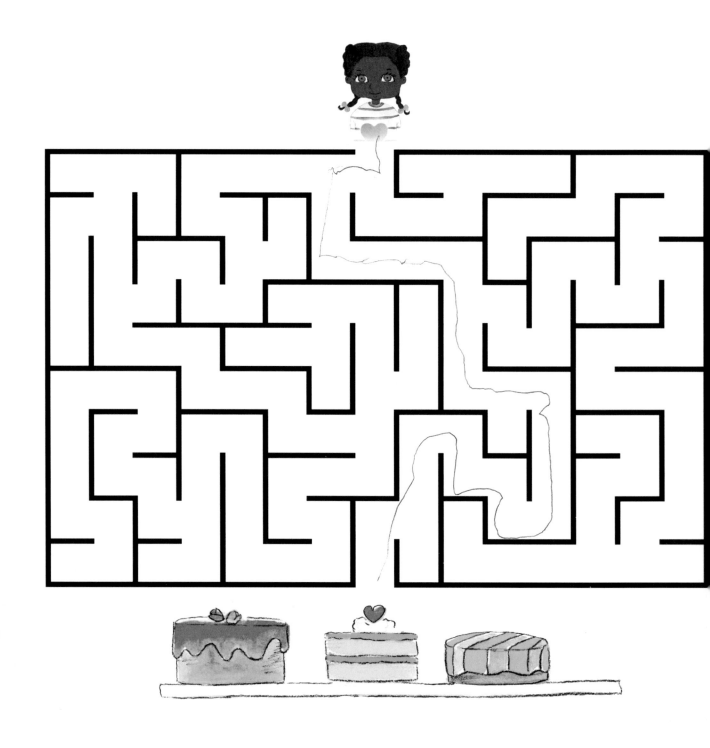

Chocolatey Brown Affirmations

I am a child of God.

I am confident.

I am beautiful.

I am unique.

I am special.

I am brave.

I am smart.

I believe in myself

I love myself.

I was created with a purpose.

I will achieve greatness.

I am me.

I am Chocolatey Brown!

Everyday look into the mirror and admire your beautiful shade of brown.
Believe with great confidence that your brown is indeed beautiful.

© Chantal Jones Productions

Meet the Author

Hi, I'm Stephanie Fleary, the author of *Chocolatey Brown*. My family originates from Grenada in the Caribbean and I currently live in Brooklyn, NY. I have been a teacher for over 10 years and I love teaching children new things and watching them grow and change. I enjoy helping others find true beauty within themselves. The idea for *Chocolatey Brown*  came to me while teaching my second grade students about their African history. Our class discussion led us to talk about the different shades of brown skin and I noticed that some of the darker skinned girls did not like their shade of brown. Growing up in Brooklyn, I experienced being treated differently by other black people because my skin was darker than some of my friends. It did not make me feel confident and beautiful but because my family taught me to always love myself, I knew that the opinions of other people did not define my beauty. I wanted to teach my students that no matter what other people say or what they see on television, their sun-kissed skin is a blessing from God and that they are descendants of royal kings and queens. I want all of my chocolatey brown girls to know that their light, medium or dark brown skin is beautiful because God says it is.

Dear Chocolatey Brown,

Do you have a chocolatey brown experience you would like to share? Maybe you just want to let us know what you think or how you feel.

Just write to us at:

Chocolatey Brown/Stephanie Fleary

P.O BOX 340019
Brooklyn, NY 11234

I hope you enjoyed reading Chocolatey Brown as much as I enjoyed writing it.

You Are Beautiful!

Stephanie Fleary